To my grandmother,

_____,

from _____

I love you because . . .

_____

_____

_____

_____

_____ ____, _____
Date

I Love My Grandmother Because . . .

Compiled by
Carolyn J. Booth
and Mindy B. Henderson

RUTLEDGE HILL PRESS®
Nashville, Tennessee

Published by Rutledge Hill Press®, Inc., 211 Seventh Avenue
North, Nashville, Tennessee 37219. Distributed in Canada
by H. B. Fenn & Company, Ltd., 34 Nixon Road, Bolton,
Ontario L7E 1W2. Distributed in Australia by Five Mile
Press Pty, Ltd., 22 Summit Road, Noble Park, Victoria 3174.
Distributed in New Zealand by Tandem Press, 2 Rugby
Road, Birkenhead, Auckland 10. Distributed in the United
Kingdom by Verulam Publishing, Ltd., 152a Park Street
Lane, Park Street, St. Albans, Hertfordshire AL2 2AU.

Typography by Compass Communications, Inc.

Design by Bateman Design
Illustrations by Farrar Hood

ISBN: 1-55853-669-8

Printed in the United States of America

1 2 3 4 5 6 7 8 9—02 01 00 99 98

Introduction

There will always be a special connection between a grandmother and her grandchildren. Our grandmothers give us unconditional love and wisdom learned throughout their lives. Sometimes they let us break rules and do things our parents don't usually allow! Whenever grandmothers and grandchildren spend time together, there will be a lot of love, a lot of fun, and a lot of precious memories to be treasured forever.

In this book, grandchildren of all ages share their special reasons for loving their grandmothers. Their words come from the heart. Some smile with joy when remembering happy times spent with their grandmothers, others' eyes fill with tears as they recall loving memories of a grandmother who is no longer with them.

Your own unique bond with your grandmother is very special. When you think about the reasons why you love your grandmother, write them down. Tell her how much you love her and why she is so precious to you. Give her a kiss and a big hug and spend some more time together making memories.

*B*eing a grandmother ranks right up there with becoming a mother, only more fun and less work!

I Love My Grandmother Because . . .

She makes me feel important.

We have family hugs with her
and Pop.

She has the most beautiful voice
and sings the sweetest songs.
She lives far away and sends me
tapes of her singing.

She doesn't mind buying the cereal
that I see on television.

She puts magic cream on my boo-
boos and makes the hurt go away.

*H*ave you ever asked yourself why your parents' mothers are called your grandmothers? Of course you haven't, because everyone with a grandmother knows that grand is the perfect word.

There is a first for everything—but there is nothing that compares to becoming a grandmother for the first time!

The one thing we never
give enough of is love.

—Henry Miller

Grandchildren learn more
from modeling than they do
from advice.

*O*ne day my daughter ran into my mother's house and yelled, Let me see it!

What? asked my mother.

Your Grammy Award! You must have one!

My mother beamed. She looked at me and then gave my daughter the biggest hug. That's just for people in the music business, sweetie!

Well, you should have one, too, protested my daughter. No one deserves a Grammy Award more than my grammy!

I Love My Grandmother Because . . .

She comes to all of my ball games. Afterward, she takes me to the concession stand and lets me buy whatever I want.

She taught me to knit.

She makes yummy chocolate gravy!

When someone is mean to me, and I tell her about it, she closes her fist and says, Do you want me to give them five knuckles?

She taught me to follow my heart.

*S*ometimes on cold nights, when I curl up under the red, white, and blue bicentennial afghan that my grandmother knitted me in 1976, I think it was not so long ago that she and I were watching the celebration. I see the fireworks in the sky. I remember the twinkle in her eyes. I remember the smile on her face, and I remember holding the small, wrinkled hand that knitted the warm afghan. I think of the stories about her that I will tell my children as we cuddle beneath the blanket, and I think of the stories that my children will tell their children as the afghan moves on through the years.

$\mathcal{I}$ love my grandmother
because when my dad gets
after me, she reminds him that
I am just like him.

I Love My Grandmother Because . . .

We sit outside at night and talk
about anything I want to talk about.

She is my favorite baby-sitter.

She is a good listener.

She says that there is no one like me!
I am a masterpiece! I am special!

She always cooks my favorite food.

$\mathcal{M}$y grandmother is a role model to me. Sometimes I will catch myself telling her about different feelings that I have or changes that I am going through. Just by the way she looks at me, I can see that she has been there before. She has been down these roads. She tells me that what I am today is made up of what I have experienced in the past. I see her, and I see her experiences. She is kind and loving. I long for my experiences to teach me to be the type of woman that she is.

𝓘 love my grandmother because when I was three years old, she was telling me a very long story, and I asked her to please let her mouth go night-night! She didn't get mad, and she laughs about it to this day.

$\mathcal{M}$y grandmother is
the gem that gives sparkle
to my life.

I Love My Grandmother Because . . .

She's my sweetie pie, and I'm her sweetie pie.

She will read me my favorite story over and over and over again.

She doesn't make me take naps if I don't want to.

I can make a mistake, and it is no big deal to her. She just says, You'll do better next time.

She makes great grilled cheese sandwiches.

Children have never been
very good at listening to
their elders, but they have
never failed to imitate them.

—James Baldwin

*S*ome wise person once said that hindsight is better than foresight. That is what makes being a grandmother so wonderful! You can use all your hindsight with your grandchildren!

I love my grandmother because she tells me funny stories about my daddy when he was my age.

We're called Lolly and Pop
by our grandchildren.
Are we suckers for them?
You bet we are!

—Lanell Padgett

Children's children are a crown to the aged.

—Proverbs 17:6

∞ ∞

AS MY
Grandmother
ALWAYS SAID . . .

*I*f you see a book, a rocking
chair, and a grandchild in the same
room, don't pass up a chance to
read aloud. Instill in your grandchild a love of reading. It's one of
the greatest gifts that you can give.

—Barbara Bush

I Love My Grandmother Because . . .

She lets me rummage through her jewelry box.

She says, You are so pretty. You look just like your mother.

She is a great storyteller.

When I think of her, I can smell her
spaghetti sauce. It is the best and
so is she!

She gave me my mommy's doll.

A good grandmother
keeps the vision of beauty
and instills this hope in her
children and grandchildren.

AS MY
Grandmother
ALWAYS SAID . . .

Remember to never talk badly about
your grandchildren's parents.

Remember to create memories that
will last forever.

Remember to listen with patience.

Remember to appreciate your
grandchildren's feelings.

Remember to share your spiritual
beliefs with your grandchildren.

I Love My Grandmother Because . . .

She fixed a special room at her house for me!

She tells me I am perfect.

She gives good hugs.

🌺

She taught me about God.
I always sat by her at church.

🌺

She taught me how to
make a garden.

*A*ny great truth can—and eventually will—be expressed as a cliché—a cliché is a sure and certain way to dilute an idea. For instance, my grandmother used to say, The black cat is always the last one off the fence. I have no idea what she meant, but at one time, it was undoubtedly true.

—Solomon Short

The secret of a happy life
is to skip having children
and go directly to
the grandchildren.

—from a MOMMA cartoon by Mel Lazarus

I love my grandmother because she puts my art all over her refrigerator.

My son, age four, looked at my mother the other day and said, Gram, are you getting old? No! she replied quickly. I'm not getting older. I'm just getting happier. She smiled and winked at him.

A grandmother's stories build strength and provide a foothold for integrity, dignity, and a sense of fearlessness. They give direction, guidance, and self-respect, define limitations, and outline freedom.

—From *Walking in Moccasins*,
Museum of Northern Arizona,
Flagstaff, Arizona

Grandmothers radiate
warmth and love.
They encourage, hug, comfort,
understand, and teach us that
we are loved.

I Love My Grandmother Because . . .

She lets me brush her hair and play
beauty shop.

She spoils me rotten.

She helps me with my homework.
She knows all about math!

She tells me about her and Paw Paw's
wedding and about my mommy and
daddy's wedding.

If I need her, all I have to do is call.

*F*amilies will live on
through the stories we tell our
children and grandchildren.

$\mathcal{Y}$oung Langston Hughes curled into his grandmother's lap as she wrapped him with a bullet-riddled shawl. He stroked the tattered shawl and listened as Grandmother Langston told how her first husband, Sheridan Leary, had gone to Harper's Ferry, Virginia, in 1859. She explained that Leary, a freeman, died at John Brown's side, fighting for the freedom of others, leaving the shawl behind as a symbol of his commitment to the cause.

Through Grandmother Lang-
ston's stories, Hughes learned to be
courageous and to fight for his
beliefs. She taught him to judge a
man by his actions, not by the color
of his skin, and that all people
deserved to be free.

Langston Hughes died in 1967.
His Kansas heritage and his grandmother's stories helped shape the
words he shared with the world.

—Kansas State Historical Society

I Love My Grandmother Because . . .

She has great stuff in her attic.

She taught me to tie my shoelaces.

She is pretty and so sweet.
She loves me and all of my cousins
equally. She says we are like the
flowers in her garden. Each of us has
a unique beauty.

She has a good shoulder to cry on.

$\mathcal{M}$y grandmother had a very special recipe for rice that she handed down to me and my sisters. When she passed away, we waited a very long time before we tried to make it. Now all of us have attempted on several occasions to duplicate the recipe. It just does not taste the same! Could it be that we don't have the secret ingredient that she must have added—her special love for us? We can't be sure, but it makes perfect sense to us.

—Terasa W. Sav

*M*y grandma is in heaven, but when I do something special, my mom says, "I'm so proud of you, and Grandma would be, too."

What is unconditional love? My first remembrance of this kind of love was with my Mamie. She was my comforter, encourager, and my biggest fan. She was a retired schoolteacher and every night we she would study with me. Once, we were conjugating Latin verbs. I was so tired of practicing that I threw a little fit and stormed from the room.

Later, feeling guilty about my behavior, I walked back to her room to apologize to her.

"David," she said, "You never need to apologize to me for anything. I know you would never do anything intentionally to hurt me."

At the moment, I knew the meaning of unconditional love. She had that for me, and I for her. Isn't that a beautiful sign of a grandmother?

I Love My Grandmother Because . . .

She is very wise.

She taught me to keep scrapbooks.

She gives me bubble baths.

She helped me make my doll's clothes. That's how I learned to sew!

She helps me say my bedtime prayers.

One time I went to Grandma's house, and we made about thirty cookies in all different shapes. I took some home to my brothers, and now every time I go to Grandma's house we always make a lot of cookies.

—Brett Henry

The reason grandchildren
and grandparents get along so
well is that they have a
common enemy—parents.

$\mathcal{I}$ love my grandmother
because when I married,
she created a special
cookbook with all of her best
recipes for me.

There was an out-of-town grandmother who was dearly loved by her young grandson. Before he could even talk, he cried when she left to return home. She would always say to him, I'll be back! I'll be back! One day, as she was about to leave, he came to her with his arms outstretched, and she picked him up. He squeezed her neck, and his voice quivered through his tears: Beback? Beback? To this day she is called BeBack, and her grandson is confident that she will always be back.

—Rule Brand

I Love My Grandmother Because . . .

She loves me no matter what.

She taught me to fold napkins and
set the table.

She does funny faces to make
me laugh!

She always let me drink out of her
fine china cups when I was a child. I
am seventy years old, and I still drink
my coffee from a fine china cup.

My secrets are safe with her.

*M*y grandmother is a great guide. She has taught me to look forward to new experiences and see how bright the future is.

$\mathcal{I}$ can still picture my grandmother, pulling her rocking chair beside the table on which her old rotary phone sat. She would take her shoes off and put her feet on the air vent, which was right below the table. I can see her performing this ritual every day—calling to check on our grades, to find out how our day went, and to tell us that she loved us. She would have talked for hours if we had let her. Through her calls she touched our hearts.

AS MY

Grandmother

ALWAYS SAID . . .

Teach your children a love
of reading and you have given
them a most precious gift.

*P*icture your grandchildren as a rose garden. Some will bloom beautifully. Others will need to be thorned to grow. Garden with the warmth of a smile, with patience and love. In your later years, your life surely will be a bed of roses.

*Y*outh! Stay close to the

young and a little rubs off.

—Alan Jay Lerner

I Love My Grandmother Because . . .

She likes to have tea parties with me.

She has pictures of me all over
her house.

She is the best biscuit maker in the world.

She takes me on fun trips to places like Disney World.

She makes every holiday and birthday a very special occasion.

Big Granny told her stories
of young love and yesterdays
with Granddaddy with a
twinkle in her eye and her
special little giggle. I feel love
just remembering her.

—Deborah Andrews

In relating the blessings
that have come their way,
grandmothers teach
us gratitude.

$\mathcal{M}$y grandmother always
wanted us to call her
Dear Heart. When she held
me for the first time, she told
my mother that was the name
she wanted me to call her
because she said that I was the

nearest and dearest thing to
her heart. As the years passed,
all of the children came to
understand exactly what their
grandmother felt—because
they had the same love for her.

—Martha Johnson

$\mathcal{I}$ love my grandmother
because when she sees me, just
the look on her face says,
I love you.

I Love My Grandmother Because . . .

She comes to my school to eat lunch with me.

She encourages me to do my best and try to make the honor roll.

She buys anything that I have to sell for school.

❀

She asks her friends to order Girl Scout cookies from me.

❀

She lets me lick the beaters when she makes a cake.

*G*randmothers don't have to be smart. They just have to know how to answer questions like, "Is God married?" and "Why do dogs chase cats?"

*G*randmothers don't have to do anything but be there.

❧

*E*verybody should try to have a grandmother, especially if you don't have a TV, because grandmothers are the only adults who have time to spare.

There are many special names
for grandmothers that are really
extensions of the mothers' names.
They include Andmomma,
Othermother, and Momma2.
How special that children think
of their grandmothers as the
"other mommies" in their lives!

I love my grandmother
because she gives me what I
need when I need it . . . and
today I need ice cream.

$\mathscr{A}$ grandmother recently met her friend for lunch. She started to tell her about her granddaughter and was cut short with this remark, "Before you start, I demand equal time, and I have ten grandchildren!"

A little boy had bought his grandmother a book and wanted to inscribe the front with something really special . He racked his brain and suddenly remembered that his father had a book with an inscription that he was very

proud of. So the little boy
decided to copy it. You can
imagine his grandmother's
surprise when she opened her
book, which was the Bible,
and found it inscribed,
"To Grandma, with the
compliments of the author."

Becoming a grandmother
is like having dessert.
The best is saved for last.

$\mathcal{I}$ love my grandmother
because she has shown me
how to pause, enjoy the
moment, and see the beauty
that surrounds me.

Grandma's Hands

I reached out for the hands to hold
To guide me through the mall
My grandma took good care of me
When I was very small

And as I grew she saw in me
The things I didn't know
She always said you're good inside
Your heart will grow and grow . . .